WHEN
PRUDENCE
MEETS
PREPAREDNESS

SHAWN CLAY
and A. AMERICAN

TABLE OF CONTENTS

FOREWARD

THE PURPOSE OF THIS BOOK is to help those of us who live a preparedness lifestyle, yet like millions of Americans, are living under a monthly budget. While we would all love to run out and purchase the best prepping gear money can buy, that simply isn't an option of most of us. However, that doesn't mean that quality gear and supplies can't be had. With a little planning, there are plenty of bargains to be had that can benefit a prepper family.

I would like to thank Chris Weatherman for his input and help with this book as well. You may recognize his pen name of Angery American and his incredible Going Home series of novels. If you haven't checked them out yet, I highly encourage you to. They have been very influential in my preparedness journey. There are a series of links to his products and books in the resource section in the back of this work.

I hope that you, the reader, are able to benefit from the suggestions on the following pages. It's my sincerest hope that this book helps families like mine to be able to put back supplies for the day we all hope never comes, and stay within our monthly budget at the same time.

CHAPTER 1:
INTRODUCTION

THOSE OF US WHO HAVE been in the prepping lifestyle for some time have likely developed their own methods for obtaining the goods or services they need. However, the last decade has seen a resurgence in public interest in preparedness, and has led to a whole new crop of preppers. Ironically, as this book is being written, the Coronavirus Pandemic is sweeping through the United States, as well as the rest of the world. States are on lockdown with shelter-in-place orders and only workers deemed essential are reporting into their places of employment. When the virus began to creep into the continental United States, there was immediately a public panic (fueled in large part by the media) that led to a fury of panic-buying of essentials.

As a result, store shelves are bare in many locations, and online ordering is seeing delays ranging from several days to several weeks of many commonly-used items. Oddly enough, toilet paper has been the focus of much of this panic buying. There have been reports of fights breaking out over the last pack of toilet paper in the store. While the media focuses on each new story detailing the panic spreading throughout the land, those of us who are preppers are seeing the payoff from our chosen way of life. While there are a few items that we have to buy from time to time, my family was fairly well stocked on most items (including precious toilet paper) and were able to ride out the panic.

Many state and government officials are advising families to be able to shelter in place for up to 30 days. Families are now realizing that our just-in-time supply chain model results in many essential supplies being severely back-ordered. People who are used to going to the grocery store every few days and picking up enough food to get by are experiencing a great disruption in their routine. The result is seeing a massive resurgence in anything prepping-related. Freeze-dried survival food is sold out nearly everywhere. Books on prepared-ness are now the focus of many readers' bookshelves and e-readers. While it may be tempting for those of us who are preppers to beat our chests and feel validated that we are justified in our way of living, the fact remains that there are many people out there who are genuinely scared and worried about how to take care of them-selves and their families. It's at a time like this, we need to draw on our knowledge and help out our neighbors. While it's tempting to raise the proverbial drawbridge and camp out in our basements with our AR's and night vision, we need to exhibit some leadership and help our communities and municipalities weather this storm and, more importantly, be better prepared for whatever event may be next on the horizon.

The purpose of this book is to help those who may be new to prepping get into the lifestyle in a sensible, budget-friendly way. Far too often, new preppers will dive headfirst into the lifestyle and spend a fortune on gear and resources that they feel they must have. Often-times, one area may take precedence, such as weapons or Bug Out Bags, but we need to remind those new folks that prepping is a well-rounded lifestyle and is best embarked upon in a sensible, rational manner.

In addition, a large segment of the population lives paycheck to paycheck. For these folks, building a stockpile of supplies all at once simply isn't feasible. Many families struggle to keep the bills at bay, and putting back extra just doesn't seem to fit within the monthly budget. Our goal for this book is to show that prepping can be done with a budget-conscious approach and that while things may seem chaotic all around us, with a little bit of common sense and a calm attitude, one can begin a lifestyle of preparedness without going broke.

CHAPTER 2:
RETAIL STORES

S INCE RETAIL STORES ARE THE usual first stop for new preppers, it's important to find ways to be frugal during shopping trips. All too often, the excitement of this new journey results in buying up resources that may not be absolutely necessary in the beginning. This happens to seasoned preppers from time to time as well, as we too fall victim to the same marketing gimmicks.

The most important thing to remember when going to buy supplies to put back is to go into the store with a purpose in mind. Just like you should never grocery shop when you are hungry, lest you buy up lots of unneeded items, it's important to have a game plan when going shopping. For those wanting to build a food reserve, calculate what you or your family eat during an average week. Depending on your budget, you can double or triple that each shopping trip and build up a solid reserve of food in a relatively short time. Many preppers are familiar with the term "copy canning". This term refers to stocking up on multiples of the same item, such as canned goods, especially when the item is something that is routinely eaten by one's family. The concept is that the food intended for immediate consumption is put into the pantry, while the food intended for long term storage is put in a separate location, to be rotated through periodically to avoid spoilage.

I should also point out a mistake that many of us seasoned preppers have learned the hard way: just because it's on sale doesn't mean you have to buy it. It's easy to do; you see that sweet two-for-one deal and it makes sense at the time, so you stock up on it. Nevermind the fact that you really aren't that big of a fan of pickled pigs feet, it was on sale! Sometimes stores mark down things for a reason: nobody else wants them. While it's true that most of us will eat pretty much anything if hungry enough, if you are in a situation such as the quarantine that a large portion of the United States is experiencing now, getting a finicky kid to eat one of the 500 cans of potted meat you bought on sale will not be a pleasant experience. It's all the more reason to be purpose-minded when shopping for preparedness items.

So, now that the importance of having a plan in mind when going shopping has been established, let's take a look at the various ways that one can save money while shopping in traditional retail stores.

First of all, the traditional print version of the Sunday paper will be packed full of sale ads for all the various stores in one's region. The Sunday edition typically costs less than $2 and whether you are looking to stock up on food, drinks, clothing, or other items, this is a great place to start. Find what is the most essential at the moment and put those circulars or coupons aside first. Go through again and see if anything else jumps out to you as being beneficial to have on hand. If so, set those aside as well. Let your weekly or monthly budget dictate priorities. Half an hour of checking for coupons at your favorite stores will often pay off in the form of significant savings at the register.

If you've ever watched any of the shows about extreme couponing, it's easy to see how it can become an addiction. As a matter of fact, you can even go on Ebay and find tons of listings of coupons that have been clipped and organized into categories. If you are buying items on a consistent basis, this may be a good idea to check into. Also, grocery stores will often have coupon dispensers in certain locations, so check and see if there are any for the items you normally purchase. Once again, just don't fall into the trap of buying simply for the sake of buying.

In addition to looking for coupons, signing up for store loyalty programs oftentimes is a great way to save money. Some programs give a designated percentage off, while others give savings on different items weekly. Others will give discounts at store-owned gas stations in the parking lot. One of the best rewards programs out there seems to be the one from CVS drug stores. The program costs the user about $5 monthly and gives the user an automatic $10 reward at the beginning of every month. In addition, the user gets 20% off CVS brand health items, ranging from bandages and first aid gear to pain relievers and vitamins. It's a great way to build a supply of medical gear and over-the-counter medication. In addition, anyone who has ever shopped at CVS knows that the 100 foot long receipt usually contains additional coupons as well. Oftentimes there is a $10 off a $50 purchase coupon, which can come in handy when buying more expensive items. Many other pharmacy stores have similar programs, so check around and find out what is available in your area. In addition, many stores offer online promotions as well, such as free shipping for orders over a certain amount. Some stores also offer a store credit card. These can be quite useful as well, provided that the user is fiscally responsible with it and avoids carrying charges over from month to month. If you decide to utilize a store credit card, it's highly advisable that you pay it off in full when the monthly statement comes. Any savings you get on the items you purchased can be quickly negated by interest charges that add up from month to month.

Also, check to see if your preferred gas station features a discount or loyalty card. Here in the southeast, Mapco gas stations are popular due to their everyday savings of 3 cents per gallon using their loyalty card, and twice a week, they offer anywhere from 7 to 12 cents off per gallon when using their card. They also give additional savings to military and law enforcement. Some programs also give points for every fuel and food / drink purchase. I choose to let my points accumulate and then redeem them for a day when I am stocking up on fuel. I've gotten up to 40 cents per gallon off, which can be a substantial savings if replenishing your emergency fuel supply.

Another great way to save money is to look into buying store-brand items. Many times, the store brand is made by the same company that has the name brand. From batteries and clothing to food and drink items, shopping store brands can save the consumer quite a bit of money over time, especially when there are sales and promotional programs. When it comes to prescriptions, generics will more often than not save the consumer money as well. If you are on one or more maintenance medications, I would highly recommend asking your pharmacy if they offer 90 day or longer options. Many times, these larger prescription orders are eligible for free shipping to the consumer, sparing them from having to drive to the pharmacy once a month.

If you are the type of person who only likes to go shopping or into town occasionally, you may very well want to check and see if any wholesale clubs exist in your area. Stores such as Sam's and Costco carry items in bulk quantities and may make more sense to those who prefer to buy in monthly buckets. As with other retail stores, do your best to avoid the temptation of buying a product that you don't necessarily need just because it's on sale.

Finally, when it comes to shopping at retail stores, utilize online resources such as Brickseek.com when looking for items to add to your preparedness supplies. This online service sends daily emails on products marked down by retailers such as Walmart, Lowes, Macy's, Home Depot, Staples, etc. There are various levels of membership available, and the level of savings can be staggering, especially if a store is closing out a particular brand or style of an item. Many essential items can be had for pennies on the dollar. Brickseek allows the user to pick specific categories to search in, such as groceries, health and beauty, sporting goods, etc. It also allows the user to check the stores in their local area and get a snapshot of current inventory available. It can be a valuable resource for those looking to build a well-rounded inventory of supplies for the months and years to come.

It should be noted that the various discount dollar stores can also be an aid in building up one's preparedness supplies. As with many other retailers, many of their generics are produced in the same facilities as the name brands. In addition, many have rewards programs that can save the consumer money. However, due diligence needs to be done when shopping at dollar stores. Oftentimes, especially in regards to food and personal care items, the quantities are less than what you find in regular retail stores. That's how they are able to price their items the way they do. For instance, a dollar store bottle of ibuprofen may be priced at $1, but it may only contain 20 tablets. The ones at a regular store will cost more, but will be a better bargain due to the quantity of tablets contained in the bottle. Make sure that you are getting the best bang for your buck when shopping at these types of stores.

By utilizing the various sales and discount programs available, the budget-conscious consumer can definitely begin to build a good reserve of the items needed by their family and save money while doing so. It's advisable to check out all the various stores that you use on a weekly basis and see which programs make the most sense. If a store has only one or two items on sale that you use frequently, it may not make sense to drive all the way there, as your savings will be negated by your fuel cost. Be smart in the way you shop, and you may very well be surprised to see how much you can save.

And since we are on the subject of money, it's advisable to allocate any extra money in the budget to paying down whatever debt you may have. Credit cards, car and house payments, student loans, etc. can have a very detrimental effect on a family's budget. Paying those off in the order of least to most expensive can certainly turn a family budget around in short order. Being 100% debt free is a worthy goal for all individuals or families, whether they consider themselves preppers or not. If you are interested in learning how to save money and pay off debt, the Dave Ramsey series of books is highly recommended. His emphasis on debt-free living is the cornerstone on which many prepper's philosophies are built.

CHAPTER 3:
THRIFT STORES

WHILE THRIFT STORES MAY CONJURE up old images of disorganized clothing racks and shelves full of junk inside dimly-lit buildings, many modern thrift stores are just as nice, if not nicer, than comparable retail stores. Most towns have one or more thrift stores, and they can often be a source of great deals on clothing, shoes, outdoor gear and more. There are multiple thrift stores in my hometown and I've picked up many bargains over the years. From nearly new jackets and shoes to flashlights and emergency gear, I've been able to add to my preparedness inventories at a fraction of the price compared to purchasing new.

Most readers will be familiar with Goodwill stores, with hundreds of them scattered throughout the United States. While some of their leadership has come under fire for their handling of donations, the stores themselves can still be a great source of gear and clothing. Other organizations such as church ministries will sometimes operate thrift stores for the purpose of raising funds for their charities. Some thrift stores will have 50% off days once or twice a month, adding additional savings for the savvy consumer. Plus, there is always the chance you will stumble upon some sort of hidden treasure. As this book is being written, there was a story out of North

Carolina where a shopper at a local thrift store found a painting that turned out to be an original Savador Dali artwork. You just never know…..

If shopping thrift stores in person isn't your thing, consider shopping online. Goodwill stores have their own online shopping platform called Shopgoodwill.com. Think of it as the Goodwill version of Ebay. If you've ever thought that all the best donations never make it to the store shelves, you're right. They go on the auction site. There is pretty much a category for anything you can think of. The amount of hunting, fishing, and camping gear I've bought off this site is staggering. True bargains can be found if you are willing to do a little digging. With shipping straight to your home, what's not to love?

In addition to the standard "one stop shop" thrift store, there are also second-hand stores that are more specialized. For instance, in Chattanooga, Tennessee, there is a store called Four Bridges Outfitters that specializes in lightly used outdoors gear ranging from camping equipment to shoes and outerwear. Their Facebook page often has an item or two that they are featuring for sale and they are able to get a lot of gently-used outdoor equipment into hands that may not normally be able to afford it. In addition, some retailers such as REI have a used gear section on their website where consumers can search for all manner of outdoor gear. The company occasionally has "garage sale" events where they discount the used merchandise in order to clear out inventory. In addition, there are rebate programs where customers can accumulate points that are redeemable in store or online for gear. If you are looking to outfit a family with preparedness gear, these used-gear options can save quite a bit of money in the long run. As with any purchase, though, make sure that you practice due diligence in selecting your gear. Check the items out for any external or internal damage before laying out your hard-earned money.

Another good second-hand place to find gear and goods is your local pawn shop. Many times, the prepper community gets keyed in on the latest and greatest gear or weapons system. Just log on to any prepper community page and there will be multiple threads about why the AR is better than the AK or why 6.5 Creedmore is the cartridge to have, while others will argue that the 30.06 is the gold standard. While running all these mental exercises on the advantages or disadvantages of a certain piece of gear can be beneficial, not everyone can afford a $2000 AR or a $900 crossbow. However, for the prepper looking for a basic deer rifle or shotgun, a good deal can often be found at a local pawn shop. Getting to know the owner can also aid in getting the best deal. I've bought several higher-end rifles and handguns at a local pawn shop for around what I would have paid for a base grade gun at a big box store. Plus, if you are the type of person that loves to haggle, pawn shops can be your place to shine. Cash in hand can often lead to a handshake and a lower-priced deal. Certain times of the year are better for shopping at these establishments. Christmas, for example, can be a great time to shop as people are pawning or selling unwanted items in order to get some present money together. Time your shopping trips right, and you just might walk out with a lot more than you expected or hoped to find.

One last type of second-hand store to check out would be your local used book store. While our handheld devices such as our cell phones and Ipads can store seemingly limitless amounts of data, what happens if the power goes out? What happens if that device gets damaged or lost? People who live a preparedness lifestyle often have a "prepper library" where they collect and keep books on the various aspects of preparedness and self-reliance. My own library contains books ranging from various weaponry to primitive skills to family first aid with both conventional and alternative methods of treatment. I inherited the Foxfire series of books about life in the rural Appalachian region from my grandfather. These books are an absolute treasure trove of history and practical skills from some of the heartiest settlers in early America. If you don't like to do a lot of buying online, or you prefer to look through a book before purchasing, a used book store can be one of the most valuable resources around. Many stores will offer trade-in programs where you can bring in your own unwanted books and swap them for store credit. This can be a great way to continually supplement your prepper library. Since many preppers also take EMP's into consideration, having books around to occupy all members of your family can be a great way to stay mentally engaged and not allow boredom or despair to start creeping in.

CHAPTER 4:
SPECIALTY STORES

W HEN IT COMES TO THE preparedness lifestyle, stores that specialize in supplying and promoting the lifestyle can be a valuable resource. If you live in the southeast, Tennessee Readiness and Carolina Readiness are well known among the prepping community. Both stores are staffed by folks who live preparedness lifestyles and not only sell the goods and equipment sought after by those who are self-reliant, but they also offer classes and instruction on various topics. Store owners and staff are also there for all levels of experience, from those just starting on a path of self-reliance to people who have been living the lifestyle for decades.

Stores of this nature are great gathering places to shop and learn all under one roof. There is a definite advantage to shopping at these stores, as the advice alone is worth showing up for. Admittedly, the pricing in these stores can be a little more than you might find at a Walmart, keep in mind that you are not only supporting a local business, but you are supporting a store that is staffed by like-minded individuals who are committed to the prepping community. During this current pandemic environment, both Tennessee and Carolina Readiness have adapted their business models to both protect the health of the owners and staff as well as keep their customers supplied with the products they need during a time when supply lines are disrupted. From organizing local food exchanges where local farms can make available their products to the local community to making in-store inventory available for mail order, the folks running these specialty stores are giving service far and above the levels of a big box store.

Stores that specialize in bulk foods and cleaning supplies are also worth checking into. Restaurant supply stores can be a great source of the larger cans of fruits and vegetables and wholesale-size quantities of beans and rice and even staple items such as sugar, flour, and spices. Janitorial and Industrial Supply stores can be a wonderful resource for cleaning and disinfecting tools and agents, trash bags, paper towels, and toilet paper. In addition, many of these companies also stock bulk quantities of first aid items, emergency supplies, and fire suppression items such as extinguishers and flame-retardant blankets. Since they are sold in larger sizes, the savings can be substantial.

A related type of specialty store to restaurant supply stores that is definitely worth checking out are the storehouses run by the LDS church. For those unfamiliar with the Latter Day Saints (also referred to as Mormons), their particular theology concentrates heavily on self-sufficiency. Church members keep long term supplies of food and water in their homes at all times. In addition, the church has set up what they refer to as "Bishop's Storehouses" that are open to church members and those in the community in need. People who fall under this category pay nothing for the goods they select, with the church only requesting some sort of repayment in the form of public service. In addition, many of the stores are open to the general public as well. Further information on locations of these storehouses can be found in the resource section at the back of the book.

These storehouses also sell bulk foods as well as staples such as flour, sugar, wheat, etc. and their pricing is reported to be much less than what the average consumer would pay at a retail or wholesale club store. This allows families with limited budgets to maintain a level of food storage of up to several months. While some denominations may take issue with some of the teachings of the LDS church, this is one area that most everyone can agree on and work towards making people more self-sufficient, regardless of their socio-economic status.

The last if the specialty stores that are worth checking out are surplus stores. Here, consumers can find government and military surplus from both the United States and around the world. Their inventories can vary from month to month, depending on what their suppliers are able to source. Products ranging from surplus uniforms and footwear to medical gear and emergency preparedness items. A word of warning about surplus stores: as with any used item, it's a buyer-beware world. Since these stores are bringing in large quantities of items from various parts of the world, it's virtually a certainty that some damaged and defective items will be mixed in. When selecting surplus gear, ensure that all parts of the item are functional and that the gear won't fail you when you need it the most. All in all, if you are willing to do a little digging around and don't mind gear that's a little dirty or worn, you can certainly add some quality items to your preparedness inventory.

CHAPTER 5:
ONLINE OPTIONS / AUCTIONS

THE ADVENT OF ONLINE BUYING has revolutionized the way the American consumer makes purchases. Places like Amazon and Ebay allow us to have nearly anything we want shipped to us within a matter of days. Hard to find items are no longer quite so difficult to locate. Online buying can provide the prepper a plethora of options for stocking up on essential items. In this chapter we will look at some of the familiar, and maybe some of the unfamiliar options for the online shopper.

Everyone reading this is likely familiar with Ebay. It's a great site to search for anything from gear to food, and everything in between. Since preppers often like redundancy in their plans and gear, finding duplicates of a piece of gear that is discontinued or hard to find can sometimes be a troublesome chore. With Ebay, those items may be available in multiple formats, allowing the buyer to choose what works best for them. In addition, since it is both a buying and selling format, preppers can auction their unwanted or unneeded items in order to raise funds to purchase more of the items they do need.

When it comes to Amazon, there's probably not many people who haven't bought from them at some point.

While their quick shipping and wide selection makes shopping a breeze, there is one other advantage that preppers can definitely take advantage of. Many products offer varying repeat delivery options. From weekly to monthly, you can set up a set delivery schedule to allow you to build your prepper inventory at a rate that is conducive to your budget. It's a great option for essentials like toilet paper, non-perishable foods, bottled water, first aid supplies, OTC medications, cleaning and disinfecting supplies, AC and furnace filters, batteries, and anything else that you use on a consistent basis. Also, don't forget to take advantage of Amazon Prime Day, when there are thousands of items discounted. The laptop that this book is being written on was purchased during a previous Prime Day for less than $200. There are tons of bargains to be had, so it's a day worth saving up for.

Another great online option for preparedness-minded individuals is Etsy. While many people view Etsy as an arts and crafts website, the reality is that many interesting and useful first aid and prepper items are available by a multitude of makers. The ability to reach out to a small manufacturer and have a custom item made is a definite plus to preppers who like to have things made to their specifications. In addition, vintage items are available as well such as knives, hand tools, oil lamps, camp stoves, and all manner of outdoors gear. There are also new items such as permanent and portable wood stoves that can be found as well. Etsy allows skilled craftsmen and women to sell their wares on a platform that is on an international level.

The world of online shopping also opens up opportunities for the savvy prepper to take advantage of auctions from city and county governments as well as federal government auctions. Surplus equipment such as vehicles, furniture, electronics, and sporting goods can be found at bargain prices. Vehicles can range from tractors and ATV's to standard passenger cars, trucks, and SUV's, all the way up to heavy construction equipment and emergency response vehicles. In addition, there are also seized property auctions that allow eligible bidders to purchase firearms, knives, electronics, vehicles, and even real estate. A listing of some of the various government auction sites can be found in the resource section in the back of the book. These are great opportunities for a prepper to pick up that heavy duty pickup truck he has been wanting, a tractor for the homestead, and maybe even a diesel storage tank so that he can store fuel on site. Who knows, one might be able to pick up some land as well and turn it into a bugout location.

Another type of online auction that can benefit the prepper is that of storage unit auctions. These auctions occur when a renter has not paid their monthly fees and the storage unit management put the unit up for auction to recover their fees. While not every storage unit is going to yield unimaginable treasures, there are some home runs every now and again where the purchaser has come into items of considerable value for a marginal investment. These can be great ways for a prepper to pick up items for their inventory and to flip what they don't want for a profit and put a little money back for a rainy day. One simply has to be careful and not let the auction world become all-consuming. Many well-intentioned people have gotten into serious financial hardship due to auctions of this type. With the exception of storage unit auctions, which are mainly sight unseen, most online auctions will feature pictures of the whole catalog that is available, giving the prospective bidder a clear indication of what is available. This helps the budget-minded prepper to hone in on what auction items would be of the maximum value for their family.

CHAPTER 6:
THE BARTER SYSTEM

I N ITS SIMPLEST TERMS, BARTERING can be defined as trading goods or services for other goods or services, without using cash as a medium. It's one of the oldest forms of exchange, being utilized by ancient civilizations before any type of money was invented. The native peoples of North America were widely known to have a barter-based economy. Tribes who were proficient in hunting and trapping would often trade meat and pelts to tribes who were proficient in making tools such as stone axes and arrow and spear points. Other examples involved trading crops and other edibles for hunting lands. Both parties traded something for something else they found of equal value. Bartering also was a key component in the survival of many families during the Great Depression here in the United States. Since money was very difficult to come by for a majority of people, the exchange of services for goods or other services became commonplace. Bartering is a great way of obtaining goods or services that one may otherwise not have the financial means to make a reality. In this day and age, there are two ways to go about bartering. The first would be a deal struck between two individuals and the second would be through the use of a barter club or service.

Personally, I have found that bartering is a great way to get into some great spots for hunting and fishing. Living here in far NW Georgia, a lot of the greatest places to hunt and fish that are located on private property. One of those prime places just happens to be located about 10 minutes from my house. It's about 40 acres that is surrounded by farms and bordered on the back by a mountain. There is also about a one acre lake full of fish. I got to know the property owner and struck a deal where I help him control the varmint population (beavers, etc) that tend to wreak havoc on the pond and surrounding creeks and also cutting and removing downed trees along with keeping the property clean in general in exchange for unlimited access to fish and hunt. Not a bad deal at all. I spend a few days a year working on his land and get to hunt and fish at my leisure. With this one agreement, I could realistically provide all the meat and fish that my family would need to sustain us. The property has abundant whitetail deer, turkey, rabbit, and squirrel, not to mention the bass, catfish, and panfish that call the lake home. The deal I struck with the property owner is a wonderful example of how the barter system works. My labor in exchange for land and lake access. Seems like a pretty good deal to me! A lot of the hunting clubs around here charge several thousands of dollars per year to hunt deer or turkey, so this arrangement saves me from having to spend a lot of money.

Other barter exchanges that can be found are swapping a percentage of a harvest for being able to farm on someone else's land, swapping mechanic work on vehicles for cleaning services, swapping yard work for a piece of lawn equipment, and swapping extra or no longer needed gear for a piece of gear that would be more useful. In each one of these exchanges, not one penny in cash was required. For people with particular skill sets, such as an auto mechanic or someone skilled in growing food, the sky is the limit on what those skill sets can be bartered for.

In addition to person to person barter arrangements, there are also organizations that help arrange transactions between individuals or groups. There are many different barter organizations in the United States alone, and the advent of the internet has allowed bartering to become a worldwide possibility. In the back of this book, you will find several different websites to help you find out more about how bartering works and how to connect with others who offer goods or services your family may need. A quick search of the internet found barter clubs and websites that specialize in the following:

- Home and Office Space
- Clothing and Footwear
- Transportation
- Entertainment
- Professional Skills
- Real Estate

The fact is, whatever your interests are, there is likely a barter club that can help you obtain it. Bartering clubs will vary in how they operate, but the basic tenet is that they charge a fee to become a member of the club. Once membership is approved and verified, the user is free to advertise his goods or services that he has to offer, and what he is looking for in return. The barter club will often help to facilitate a match between what the user is seeking and another member that has that good or service to offer. When a deal is struck, another fee may be assessed from one or both parties. And while many people assume that barter clubs may be great for finding services such as mechanic work, cleaning services, or gear such as electronics and sporting goods, many barter clubs have services such as medical care, real estate services, and legal services. For individuals or families who are looking to expand their preparedness inventories or skill sets and are working with limited funds, the barter concept may be able to help them obtain the goods and services they need.

CHAPTER 7:
LOCAL BARGAINS

WHEN LOOKING TO ADD TO your preps at a bargain price, don't overlook the resources that may be within your own neighborhood or merely a short drive away. In my neck of the woods, weekends mean garage and estate sales. I can admit that these types of sales are one of my guilty pleasures. Over the years, I've found countless items that I bought not only because they were a bargain, but also because they filled an empty spot in my preps. Last year, I was fortunate enough to come across an ad for an estate sale for a man who was a diehard prepper. I picked up a huge assortment of current and recently-expired medical supplies, along with some other survival items for a fraction of what I would have spent if purchased from a retail store. The icing on the cake was when the lady running the estate sale asked me if I would be interested in some MRE's. I told her that I certainly would be, depending on the price. She told me that they had several cases that they were needing to move out of the basement, as the house was being sold as well. She explained that they were expired, but if I wanted them, I could have them for free as long as I took all of them. I happily pulled around to the basement to be greeted by a small storage room off to the side that had a wall of shelves filled with cases of MRE's. In total, I wound up with

12 full cases and a few partials. The best part was, they were only a year or two expired. They had been kept in a cool, dry location, so they were still good to go. It was definitely my best score to date.

If you are interested in checking out your local garage sales and estate sales, there are numerous ways to find out what's available in your area. Most cities have those free classified ad papers that have several pages of garage sales listed. In addition, most local newspapers will have a classified section that lists the upcoming sales by city or community. There are websites as well that can help you hone in on the sales that will be the best bang for your buck, as many people like to specify the goods that they will have available. Some of those websites can be found in the resource section at the back of this book. I tend to look for sales that feature key words such as hunting, camping, sporting goods, outdoors, etc. Many people who frequent these types of sales will build a map of the locations of the sales they want to hit and go about it in the most efficient manner. The best bargains are had at the very beginning of the sale, when all the goods are first available, but don't overlook the end of the day bargains as well, as most folks don't want to return all the goods to their garage or basement. I've picked up all manner of things by making an offer on all the remaining goods. I keep what I want and either give away or trade the other goods for things I need. Certain times of the year are better than others, such as around Christmas. During this time, people are wanting to raise money, so they often are more willing to make a deal. Watch for sales in the months following a natural disaster, such as a hurricane. People tend to panic in the days leading up to an event like this, buying up cases of bottled water and high-demand items such as generators, only to sell them for a greatly reduced price a few months later because they are tired of it taking up space in the garage.

There are also other online services that can connect buyers and sellers in practically any geographic region. Services such as Facebook Marketplace, LetGo, Mercari, OfferUp, and 5miles are just a few of the sites that can show you all the goods and services available in your community or city. I've used several of these sites throughout the years and have found that bargains are out there if you are willing to look for them. One thing to keep in mind when dealing with sites like this is that if you are meeting someone you don't know, ensure that you are meeting in a public area. Many police departments now have designated parking areas where trades and sales can be conducted under full view of cameras, thereby increasing the odds of a successful transaction. There are many people who have been scammed or even assaulted by less scrupulous individuals who prowl these sites. Due diligence is always encouraged, and the old saying of "Buyer Beware" could not be any more applicable to this situation. Do your homework and meet in a safe spot, and who knows what you might find!

Finally, don't discount the good old-fashioned flea market. While some may be turned off by the prospect of going to these types of places, the simple fact is that bargains can certainly be found if one simply takes the time to stroll up and down the aisles. Like thrift stores, they can be a great source of stocking up on clothing and footwear in larger sizes for kids to grow into, along with tools, electronics, sporting goods, and locally-grown produce. Some larger flea markets even have farm animals such as chickens, guineas, goats, and ducks for sale. Price haggling is pretty much expected at these places, so they are great venues for practicing your negotiating skills as well.

CHAPTER 8:
NATURE'S RESOURCES

W HEN LOOKING TO LIVE A preparedness lifestyle on a budget, we must consider all the resources at our disposal in the world around us. Nature has everything that we need to sustain ourselves if we simply know where to look and how to attain it. It also provides ample opportunity to expand our skill sets and strengthen both our bodies and minds, while at the same time saving money in our monthly budgets.

When it comes to providing food for our families, nature definitely rises to the occasion. From small and large game hunting to fishing to foraging wild edible plants, the resources available in our wild places are second to none. With various hunting seasons essentially spanning the entire year, a skilled hunter can fill up the freezer with small game such as squirrel and rabbit, birds such as dove, pheasant, duck, goose, and turkey, and large game such as deer, elk, moose, antelope, and bear. With different seasons for archery, primitive weapons, and modern weapons, a hunter can become proficient in many different ways of taking wild game. Some states even allow the taking of small game with high power air rifles, allowing folks who may not be comfortable with traditional firearms the opportunity to participate in the hunt as well. It should be noted that the proper hunting licenses will need to be purchased in order to take the various types of game. The money generated by the purchase of hunting and fishing licenses helps to maintain and increase habitat for the public to enjoy, as well as investing in the health and restoration of animal numbers in areas that have been over-harvested in the decades past.

When taking game, especially large game, the hunter has the opportunity to learn to utilize as much of the animal as possible. From the organs and meat to the hide itself, there are tons of uses for the resources that these animals provide. In addition to the animals hunted for food, there are also a number of animals that can be trapped for their fur and meat. Animals such as beavers, mink, and other fur-bearing animals are highly sought after and can bring in significant money for the dedicated trapper. Since trapping is a passive activity, the trapper can set an entire series of traps and then check them on a regular basis to ensure that the animals caught are dispatched humanely and that the fur and meat are not ruined from staying in the elements too long. Trapping, like hunting, allows the outdoorsman to learn the habits and quirks of these animals. Like any other skill, it takes time to master, but definitely pays off for the dedicated student.

Lastly, consider if your state has an invasive species such as wild hogs. These animals have become a nuisance throughout the country due to their destructive rooting nature and their ability to rapidly reproduce. In some states, there is no season or limit on hunting or trapping hogs, which could be a godsend to the prepper looking to put back large quantities of meat. Here in the southeast, hogs are so prevalent that many landowners will pay to have hunters come in and cull the numbers. This allows a savvy hunter to not only procure food for their family and friends, but they can make some good side money as well. The same goes for many animals deemed nuisances, such as coyotes. Farmers who specialize in livestock operations will often hire hunters or trappers to come in and eradicate as many coyotes as possible, because of the detrimental effect the animals have on their calves and mothers. Lots of predator hunting is done at night, allowing the hunter to have an after-hours method of bringing in additional income.

Fishing is another way the prepper can provide food for their family. It's also a great activity to do as a family. From the oceans to the tiniest creeks, there are a myriad of aquatic creatures that can be caught or trapped in order to go on the supper table. One caveat to fishing, especially in inland rivers and lakes is to be aware of any pollution warnings for specific species. There may be restrictions on which species are deemed edible, some with warnings on how many pounds per month are deemed safe for eating. Certain sections of rivers and creeks may also be deemed as "off limits" for the purposes of fishing for consumption. Since waterways have always been associated with industries, there have been tons of pollutants dumped into them over the last hundred years or more. While environmental cleanups have seen amazing progress, many areas in the southeast still have warnings for mercury in lakes and rivers. Signs around popular fishing spots will usually tell how much fish can be safely consumed if caught out of the surrounding area. It's a sobering reminder of how we as humans need to do a better job of being good stewards of the resources around us.

Fishing, like trapping, offers the outdoorsman the opportunity to set out nets and trotlines, along with jug fishing, where hooks and lines are set out that are attached to jugs or soda bottles and recovered a day or two later, often miles away from their starting point. As with hunting regulations, be sure to abide by local rules and ordinances and have the proper licenses to be able to use public areas. In many states, there are certain days in the summer that are designated as free fishing days to the general public in all state or federal waters. These days are wonderful opportunities to introduce the sport of fishing to those who may not have ever considered its usefulness as part of a preparedness lifestyle.

In addition to hunting, fishing, and trapping, nature also provides a vast amount of edible plants. From the various types of mushrooms found in the forest to the weeds such as dandelions and clover that we find in our yards to wild berries to edible tree barks, nature provides a myriad of options for the educated forager. With uses for both food and medicinal purposes, the value of plants should not be overlooked. Plants do not require hunting or trapping, only collecting. They do not require specialized tools and, in most cases, only require one's hands to collect and prepare. Plants are a great way to stretch a meal, too. While Americans often make meat or fish the main ingredient in a meal, in many parts of the world, meat is used more as a seasoning agent in a meal, often due to price or scarcity. The addition of locally-sourced edible plants can make a meager meal into one that is much more filling.

A word of caution in this area, though. There are many plants that are toxic in varying levels to humans if consumed. It is highly advised that anyone interested in learning about edible plants to seek the counsel of an instructor who is well versed in the field, along with independent research through books and established websites. If you've been a fan of the series Alone on the History Channel, you've seen just how important foraging can be in survival situations. Participants such as Alan Kay and Nicole Apelian are well versed in wild edibles and even offer occasional classes on the subject. I've spoken with people who have attended Alan Kay's "weed walks" and they found the experience to be an overwhelmingly positive and valuable one.

In addition to wild edible foraging, don't overlook the backyard garden. With the recent Coronavirus outbreaks resulting in people spending extended periods of time staying at home, the concept of the home garden has seen and incredible resurgence. Entire Youtube channels are dedicated to growing a wide variety of fruits and vegetables in minimal spaces. In addition, growing herbs and spices can be done in spaces as small as the kitchen window. Some of the more popular channels can be found in the resource section at the back of this book. Both myself and Angery American have home gardens and I recently built a large composting box where we put coffee grounds and different food and plant waste to create rich soil for our raised beds. And since I have a son who is an avid fisherman just like myself, the added benefit of having a virtual worm farm within our compost pile is simply an added bonus.

Composting can also be a great visualization of the concept that nothing in nature is wasted. In this case, worms are prevalent in compost to aid in the breakdown of organic matter. These worms are then collected for the next fishing outing. The fish caught on these worms are eaten in future meals, and the carcasses are added to the compost pile, which starts the process all over again. Getting the whole family involved in starting and maintaining a compost pile is a great way to teach the concepts of sustainability and responsible use of resources. For the record, I suggested that Chris allow me to record him singing "The Circle of Life" from the movie The Lion King and include it as a bonus link in the resource guide, but that idea was quickly and definitively squashed.

Finally, never underestimate the ability of mother nature to provide a whole-body fitness center. In a time where the term "social distancing" is everywhere, we are just now seeing a lot of parks and public recreation areas reopen in a limited capacity, while many gyms and health clubs remain closed. Getting out and hitting a walking trail for a few miles will give your body a wonderful cardiovascular workout, as well as getting some fresh air in your lungs and vitamin D on your skin from the sun. Going on a hiking trip with a backpack will work every major muscle group in the body, as well as giving one an opportunity to practice living off the land and essentially giving a "dry run" to a bug-out scenario. Far too many preppers build get-home bags and bug-out bags, only to have them sit in the closet. Many of these preppers would be in for a rude awakening if they ever have to throw those packs on and get out of town quickly. Take your gear out for a test run. Get out in nature and survive for a weekend. It's a wonderful way to see what really is important in your pack and what can be discarded or condensed.

Being in nature also helps the mind. Studies have proven that time spent in the outdoors can help to "reset" our bodily rhythms. A 48-hour trip where the phones are turned off and stowed in the pack can be a godsend to the busy person who never takes the time to disconnect. In addition, there are many books and dissertations on the importance of allowing children to spend time in the outdoors. Mother Nature provides all that we, as humans, need for not only our physical survival, but for our mental and spiritual well-being too. Find a way to enjoy it. Whether you are a hiker, trail runner, mountain biker, hunter, fisherman, kayaker, or camper, go out and enjoy the outdoors. Just make sure to always let others know your destination and intended return time, building in a little extra time just in case you want to explore that spur trail or stop for the evening at a particularly scenic area. That way, should you get lost or injured, there will be a predetermined time that your friends or relatives will notify search and rescue resources. Also, ensure that you carry a small survival kit that will allow you to cover the essentials such as fire, shelter, first aid and water purification. The more time we spend in nature, the more important it's preservation for future generations will be to those of us who enjoy it's bounty.

CHAPTER 9:
VEHICLE OPTIONS AND CONSIDERATIONS

T HE PURCHASE OF A VEHICLE is not something to be taken lightly. In most cases, it's a significant allotment of funds. While we would all love to have the latest and greatest in luxury and comfort, or perhaps off-road ruggedness, the fact remains that we all have a budget to work with. To start with, I would advise strongly against going into debt for a vehicle. While it may be tempting to work that monthly payment into your budget, there are any number of circumstances that will turn that payment into a burden. The recent coronavirus pandemic has seen a lot of Americans lose their jobs. As a result, discretionary income has been slashed. A quick drive past some of the credit unions and banks in my hometown reveals many newer-model vehicles with "for sale" signs in their windows. Miss one or two payments, and that new vehicle is no longer yours.

While I'm not advocating that everyone drive an '82 Datsun, I'm definitely advocating that people truly consider their needs and take a long-term approach when considering the purchase of a vehicle. Since a new vehicle depreciates significantly as soon as the tires hit the pavement outside the dealership, many people opt to purchase a vehicle with a few thousand miles and, in turn, save several thousand dollars. Due diligence is always necessary when purchasing a new to you vehicle. With the availability of all the pros and cons of your preferred vehicle at your digital fingertips, it's easy to weigh your options. Picking a vehicle that has the right combination of reliability, durability, and cost of repairs can save you a lot of money in the long run.

Since many preppers prefer to work on things themselves, older vehicles can hold a particular allure. While the advent of computerized systems in newer vehicles can certainly make our drive time more comfortable, when one of those systems fails, it can be extremely frustrating, and often very expensive to repair. For that reason, many preppers will take the route of having one more modern, family-style vehicle along with an older, more rugged "SHTF" vehicle. If you spend any time on preparedness and survival websites that discuss vehicles, you will find that there is a huge preference for pre-computer vehicles, mostly in the age range of 1980's and older. These vehicles have minimal computer controls and mostly rely on mechanically-driven systems to operate. Replacing major components can be done much more easily than on newer models. My father and uncle once bought a brand new muscle car in the 1970's. I can't recall the particular make and model, but the first thing they did was pull the motor and perform several modifications in my uncle's garage to give the car more horsepower. All the work was done by the two of them. Trying to do the same with a new car would take a team of mechanics and electronic technicians.

Working on your own vehicles also provides an opportunity to turn it into a family affair. I can remember helping my dad and grandfather work on their older Ford and Dodge trucks they owned while I was growing up. All of the repairs were pretty straight-forward and I was able to learn some of the mechanical processes that powered the vehicles. My father and grandfather were firm believers that, at a minimum, a vehicle owner should be able to perform basic functions such as changing the oil, using booster cables to jump off a battery, air up tires, checking and topping off all fluid levels, and changing a flat tire.

In my own humble opinion, it's hard to beat the ruggedness of a 1970's or 80's K5 Blazer or Bronco or the versatility of a crew cab, long bed F250 with the powerful 460 V8 motor. While they may not provide the best fuel economy, they certainly make up for it in versatility and raw power. If you are looking for something to serve as an EMP-proof vehicle, there are a number of options that will keep you moving long after the freeways are clogged with non-functioning, computer-controlled new model vehicles. Whether your choice is a rugged 4x4 to get to your hunting camp or bug-out location, or more along the lines of a classic ride like a VW Bug or a classic muscle car like a Mustang or Camaro, there is a wealth of information available to handle the most minor repair to the most complicated overhaul. Prices for replacement parts typically are lower, and the availability of aftermarket parts or junkyard inventory are much higher. Manuals from companies such as Haynes and Chilton are available that show exploded diagrams of every major vehicular component, as well as part names and numbers. They are an invaluable resource to the well-read prepper. Since I have a side business that sells vintage pocket knives and sporting goods, I'm always searching through antique stores and estate sales. I come across vehicle repair manuals from time to time and always buy them, as they are typically only priced at a few dollars. Over the years, I've begun to amass a decent library of vehicle service manuals. Even though I don't personally own many of the vehicles I have manuals for, my thought is that they can be a valuable reference source should the grid ever go down, as they can be bartered for other needs or services or even contributed to a community resource library.

As far as options on your vehicles go, the sky is truly the limit. Depending on the age of your vehicle, it's easy to add pretty much whatever creature comfort you desire. However, there are a few features that I definitely recommend. First would be an adequate, functioning heater. I live in Georgia, and summers can be brutal without air conditioning in a vehicle, I've gotten by for many years in various vehicles that I've owned. However, we do sometimes get some extremely cold weather that brings snow and ice storms with it. In these cases, not having heat can be deadly. Several people suffered from hypothermia and a few died from exposure during an ice storm that hit the Atlanta region a few years ago after their cars ran out of gas and they froze to death. Another feature I would recommend would be an automatic transmission on any vehicle that will be operated by multiple family members. While the knowledge of driving a manual transmission is definitely essential, if a vehicle is having to be driven by someone in an emergency situation, not having to manipulate the clutch and shifter can take some of the stress out of the situation. I would also advocate for some sort of towing package. Whether towing a camping trailer out to the lake or taking supplies to your bug-out location, the ability to pull a trailer can effectively double or triple the amount of supplies you can haul. Finally, I would select tires that are at least rated as "All Terrain". While not all of us will go into the backwoods trails or enjoy a good mudding session, any vehicle should be able to navigate mild off-road terrain successfully. Rainy and snowy weather can also make conditions hazardous, so the proper tire can make a lot of difference between getting home safely and winding up stuck in a ditch. I would also ensure that any vehicle that is a daily driver have at least one tow hook attachment for recovery purposes.

Regardless of if you chose a vehicle simply to get to work and back, or you intend for it to take you on back-country adventures, be smart about what you purchase. Make sure that, if at all possible, you pay for the vehicle in its entirety at the time of purchase. If you simply must finance, please go for the shortest term possible. Dealers will offer financing up to 84 months on some models, and the payments can appear to be quite reasonable. However, Murphy loves to make an appearance at the worst time, and you may be stuck with a payment that you can't afford, which may result in the bank taking back the vehicle. Don't fall into the trap of "justifying" frequent upgrades to the newest model of your vehicle. Most preppers I know always have an older vehicle that does duty as their weekend worker and a backup vehicle in case their daily driver is down for some reason. It's the old "two is one, and one is none" principle.

CHAPTER 10:
OTHER CONSIDERATIONS

IN CLOSING, THESE ARE ONLY a few of the suggestions of ways that you can live a preparedness lifestyle on a budget. The sky is the limit when it comes to creative ways to save money. If you truly sit down and put pen to paper, you'll see that there is almost always some flexibility in the budget, especially if you cut back on some of the most common money-wasters such as eating out everyday for lunch, that $9 morning latte, etc.

We'll leave you with a few parting ideas to save you some money. For instance, take advantage of your state's sales tax holidays. Most states have sales tax holidays around the start of the school year. While that may limit your purchases to school-related items, you could still save some money on that new laptop you have been needing, along with significant savings on clothes, shoes, and accessories. In addition, with September being designated as "National Preparedness Month", many states offer a similar sales tax holiday on prepper items such as generators, storm shelters, first aid gear, etc. If you have been considering a large purchase, this would be the ideal time to pull the trigger on it.

If you live in an area prone to evacuations (such as wildfire country or hurricane country), consider familiarizing yourself with the various hotel chains in your region. If you travel frequently, those loyalty program perks and free room rewards will come in handy if you need to evacuate for a few days, taking the financial sting out of an already stressful situation.

Don't forget to check and see if your state emergency management agency offers grants towards storm shelters and safe rooms. Many states have agreements through FEMA where they offer tax incentives and rebates to help offset the purchase of one of these items. Since big ticket items tend to carry big ticket prices, these grants can really take some of the sting out of the purchase.

Speaking of FEMA, there are a number of free courses available through the government organization's website. They cover all types of information such as incident response, preparation, community readiness, etc. In addition, most counties and municipalities have a C.E.R.T. (Community Emergency Response Team). These are volunteer groups that stand ready to backup first responders in mass casualty incidents. There are training classes available and a process to get certified. These groups provide a valuable service, and also offer an insight into the world of emergency response that most people will never have access to. Becoming a member of one of these teams can allow a prepper to expand their network, all while gaining valuable skill sets that can benefit their community during a time of crisis. All at no cost to the volunteer. It's a win-win situation no matter how you look at it!

Also keep an eye out for any retail store closings in your area. Years back, when many of the local Kmart stores were going out of business, there were tons of bargains to be had. The sporting goods section was ripe for the picking. Ammo was marked down, the camping gear was greatly reduced, as was the fishing gear. In situations like this, the good items sell out quickly, so take advantage of a store closing sale as soon as you can. You'll likely be surprised at what you can find.

A great time to save on gear is at the changing of the seasons. When summer is transitioning to fall, bargains can be found on all sorts of outdoors gear. One of my personal favorite times is when stores such as Walmart begin clearing out the hunting gear shortly after Christmas. As with store closing sales, the best items tend to sell out fast, so if you've been holding out for that new rod and reel combo, deer rifle, patio furniture set, lawn mower, or any other big purchase, you'd be well advised to check out the end of season clearances at your local big box store.

Finally, consider what is arguably the best method of all to save money: work with what you've got. It's always tempting to want to upgrade to the newest model or version. "Justifying" buying a new vehicle can be fairly easy, with that all-too-convenient flexible, long-term financing. Maybe you "could" afford that house and land if you go with one of those adjustable rate mortgages. However, as has been stated before, getting out and staying out of debt is one of the best moves a prepper can make. The concept of delayed gratification can be one of the most rewarding things in life. If your goal is to buy that house and land that you want to move out of the city into, set aside as much as you can every month. Also, make sure you keep your current residence in as nice shape as possible. The nicer it is, the more it will bring when it's time to make that move.

If your vehicle is in good shape, keep it going on down the road by maintaining a proper maintenance schedule. There will always be a newer and better vehicle available, so resist that urge to hit the car lot. If you have a decent firearm setup, your money would be best spent on ammo and training rather than chasing the newest caliber or weapon platform. Internet forums are full of opinions on what's best and why you should choose Brand A over Brand B. It can be easy to get caught up in all the debate while losing focus on what's really important. I once read the quote that a first rate rifleman with a second rate rifle will always beat out a second rate rifleman with a first rate rifle. It's not always fun, and it may seem like torture at times, but working with what you have will help your budget along, and you'll also find ways to get the most out of your current setups.

RESOURCE GUIDE

This section will give you, the reader, some valuable information on how to put into practice the concepts covered in the book, along with pages to make notes on when considering purchases, cataloging inventory, etc, along with some articles that you might find helpful.

COUPON SAVINGS

A quick search of **Ebay** for coupons came up with the following results.

https://www.ebay.com/sch/i.html?_from=R40&_trksid=p2380057.m570.l1313.TR12.TRC2.A0.H0.Xcoupons.TRS0&_nkw=coupons&_sacat=0

Here's a few other sites that offer info and coupons for a variety of brands and stores.

https://thekrazycouponlady.com/
https://www.savings.com/
https://www.coupons.com/
https://www.couponmom.com/
https://www.joinhoney.com/

Also, companies such as **Rakuten** offer rebate programs that help you build cash back as you purchase items.
https://www.rakuten.com/

Definitely check out **Brickseek**. Covering a variety of stores such as Walmart, Target, and Lowe's, the savings can add up in a hurry! Various membership levels are available, including a free membership. This is one of my favorite websites, as it has saved me a lot of money and helped add to my prepping stores.
https://brickseek.com/

GROCERY STORE LOYALTY PROGRAMS

Winn Dixie
https://www.winndixie.com/rewards

Food City
https://www.foodcity.com/savings-rewards/valucard/

Bi-Lo
https://www.bi-lo.com/rewards-logged-out

Albertsons
https://www.albertsons.com/justforu-guest.html

Kroger
https://www.kroger.com/d/kroger-rewards-debit-card

Piggly Wiggly
https://www.shopthepig.com/rewards-card

Save A Lot
https://savealot.com/email

Food Lion
https://www.foodlion.com/promotions/shop-and-earn/

ARTICLES ON "COPY CANNING"

https://www.stockupfood.com/
food-storage-by-copy-canning/
http://floridahillbilly.com/copy-canning/

PHARMACY STORE LOYALTY PROGRAMS

CVS
https://www.cvs.com/carepass/join
https://www.cvs.com/extracare/home

Walgreens
https://www.walgreens.com/balancerewards/balance-rewards.jsp

Rite Aid
https://www.riteaid.com/wellness/wellness-rewards

GAS STATION LOYALTY PROGRAMS

Mapco
https://www.mapcorewards.com/

Exxon
https://www.exxon.com/en/rewards-program

BP / Amoco
https://www.bp.com/en_us/united-states/home/prod-ucts-and-services/our-rewards.html

Shell
https://www.fuelrewards.com/

Marathon
https://www.makeitcount.com/

Conoco
https://www.conoco.com/cards-and-rewards

Racetrac
https://www.racetrac.com/Rewards/RaceTrac-Rewards

Raceway
http://www.racewaypetroleum.com/

Speedway
https://www.speedway.com/speedy-rewards

Sunoco
https://www.sunoco.com/rewards

Circle K
https://www.circlek.com/easyrewards

Phillips 66
https://www.phillips66gas.com/cards-and-rewards

Wawa
https://www.wawa.com/about-wawa-rewards

Maverick
https://www.maverik.com/rewards/

TRAVEL CENTER LOYALTY PROGRAMS

Pilot / Flying J
https://pilotflyingj.com/rewards/

Petros
https://www.ta-petro.com/ultraone

Love's Travel Centers
https://www.loves.com/en/my-love-rewards

WHOLESALE CLUBS

Sam's Club
https://www.samsclub.com/

Costco
https://www.costco.com/

Boxed.com
https://www.boxed.com/

SPORTING GOODS STORES LOYALTY PROGRAMS

Bass Pro Shops / Cabelas
https://www.basspro.com/shop/en/points

Gander Outdoors
https://www.ganderoutdoors.com/join-goodsam

Sportsman's Warehouse
https://www.sportsmans.com/apply

Scheels
https://www.scheels.com/visacard

DOLLAR STORE LOYALTY PROGRAMS

Dollar General
https://dg.coupons.com/rewards/

Family Dollar
https://www.familydollar.com/smart-coupons-app

Dollar Tree
https://www.dollartree.com/
online-faq-value-seekers-club

FINANCIAL ADVICE

Dave Ramsey
In addition to his daily radio show, Dave's website has a ton of resources available to help in your debt reduction journey.
https://www.daveramsey.com/

Clark Howard
The guru of frugal living, Clark's website offers a wealth of valuable info.
https://clark.com/

Crown Financial Ministries
Founded by Larry Burkett, this organization follows a Christian approach to all things financial.
https://www.crown.org/

THRIFT STORE LOCATORS

Thriftigo
https://www.thriftigo.com/

Thrift Store Listings
http://www.thriftstorelistings.com/

Thrift Shopper
http://www.thethriftshopper.com/

Goodwill Store Finder
https://www.gwoutletstoreloca-
tor.com/local-thrift-stores/

Shop Goodwill
This Ebay-style auction site has items from Goodwill stores located nationwide. With categories such as electronics, clothing, and sporting goods, there's something for everyone. This is another personal favorite of mine.
https://www.shopgoodwill.com/

USED CAMPING / SPORTING GOODS STORES

Four Bridges Outfitters
http://www.fourbridgesoutfitters.com/

REI Co-Op
https://www.rei.com/used
https://www.rei.com/promotions/garage-sale
https://www.rei.com/membership/
dividend#dividendFAQ

Geartrade
https://www.geartrade.com/?gclid
=EAIaIQobChMIoY2SnOCH6wI
Vk-DICh1xpQ2_EAAYASAAEgLGxfD_BwE

OutdoorsGeek
https://www.outdoorsgeek.com/product-category/
buy-now-used/

PAWN SHOP FINDERS

National Pawnbrokers Association
https://nationalpawnbrokers.org/
member-directory/#!directory/map

Pawn Guru
https://www.pawnguru.com/

Pawn Shop Listings
https://www.pawnshoplistings.com/

PawnShops.Net
http://www.pawnshops.net/

DISCOUNT BOOK STORES

While online info is great, and we have Google and other search engines at our fingertips, what happens if the grid goes down? Having a well-rounded prepper library can be a gamechanger in such a situation. Here are some sources where you can build that library at a discount.

Book Outlet
https://bookoutlet.com/?source=ppc&ppc_campaign=
g1040978058&gclid=EAIaIQobChMI0cnbwOOH6w
IVA6_ICh04VwyZEAAYAiAAEgILdfD_BwE

Second Sale
https://www.secondsale.com/?gclid
=EAIaIQobChMI0cnbwOOH6wI-
VA6_ICh04VwyZEAAYAyAAEgKhevD_BwE

Thrift Books
https://www.thriftbooks.com/

Alibris
https://www.alibris.com/discount-books

Book Depot
https://www.bookdepot.com/

McKay's Used Books
http://www.mckaybooks.com/

SPECIALTY STORES

Carolina Readiness
https://carolinareadiness.com/

Tennessee Readiness
https://www.tennesseereadiness.com/

Emergency Essentials
https://beprepared.com/?gclid=EAIaIQobChMIt-vjou-
WH6wIVluDICh0OXw7_EAAYASAAEgL_v_D_BwE

Blue Monster Prep

https://bluemonsterprep.com/

RESTAURANT SUPPLY STORES

https://www.webstaurantstore.com/locations/
tennessee/chattanooga-restaurant-supply/
https://www.therestaurantstore.com/
https://www.katom.com/

JANITORIAL AND INDUSTRIAL SUPPLY STORES

https://www.roll-aidindustrial.com/
https://www.cleanitsupply.com/c-2306/janitorial-
supplies.aspx
http://www.conceptsupply.com/janitorial-cleaning-
supplies.html
https://www.grainger.com/category/
cleaning-and-janitorial
https://www.wholesalejanitorialsupply.com/

LDS STOREHOUSES

These locations are a great way to stock up on long-term
emergency food.
https://providentliving.churchofje-
suschrist.org/food-storage/
home-storage-center-locations-map?lang=eng

AMAZON SAVINGS

Repeat Order Program
https://www.amazon.
com/b?ie=UTF8&node=15283820011

Amazon Prime Day Info
https://www.amazon.com/primeday

ETSY

This site is great for finding preparedness and emergency items that you may not find anywhere else. Lots of small, independent stores sell here and you are helping keep small businesses moving forward. Here is an example of some emergency preparedness items available.
https://www.etsy.com/search?q=emergency%20 preparedness

GOVERNMENT SURPLUS AUCTION SITES

From generators to vehicles to office supplies, government auctions can yield a wide variety of items.

All Surplus
https://www.allsurplus.com/

GovPlanet
https://www.govplanet.com/

GovDeals
https://www.govdeals.com/

Public Surplus
https://www.publicsurplus.com/sms/browse/home

STORAGE UNIT AUCTION SITES

StorageAuctions.com
https://storageauctions.com/

SelfStorageAuction.com
https://www.selfstorageauction.
com/storage-auctions-near-me/
show_auctionSearch/type_online

Cube Smart Self Storage
https://www.cubesmart.com/storage-auctions/

Storage Treasures
https://www.storagetreasures.com/

Storage Unit Auction List
https://www.storageunitauctionlist.com/

BARTER CLUBS AND INFO

Barter News
http://barternews.com/barterclubs.htm

Bartering Website Guide
https://www.moneycrashers.com/
best-bartering-swapping-websites/

Southern Barter Club
https://southernbarterclub.com/

Bartering Sites and Articles

https://electronics.howstuffworks.com/family-tech/
tech-for-parents/online-bartering-websites-tips.htm
https://www.iscripts.com/
blog/15-most-popular-barter-exchange-networks/
https://www.barteronly.com/
http://www.barterquest.com/

ESTATE SALE WEBSITES

EstateSales.Net
https://www.estatesales.net/

EstateSales.Org
https://estatesales.org/

EstateSale.Com
https://www.estatesale.com/

Everything But The House
https://www.ebth.com/

Mega Estate Sales
https://www.megaestatesales.com/

GARAGE SALE WEBSITES

Garage Sale Finder
https://garagesalefinder.com/yard-sales/by-zip/

Garage Sales, Yard Sales, & Estate Sales
https://gsalr.com/

YardSales.Net

https://yardsales.net/

Post My Garage Sale
https://postmygaragesale.com/

VarageSale.Com
https://www.varagesale.com/

Craigslist
https://www.craigslist.org/about/sites

Facebook Marketplace
https://www.facebook.com/marketplace/

FLEA MARKET WEBSITES

https://sites.google.com/site/fleamarketfinderapp/
https://www.fleamarketmalls.com/
https://www.fleamarketinsiders.com/

POPULAR APPS FOR BUYING & SELLING

LetGo
https://www.letgo.com/en-us

Mercari
https://www.mercari.com/

Offer Up
https://offerup.com/

5 Miles
https://www.5miles.com/

SURVIVAL & PREPAREDNESS WEBSITES / SHOWS / YOUTUBE CHANNELS OF INTEREST

Alone
One of the few legit survival shows out there.
https://www.history.com/shows/alone

Nicole Apelian
Nicole is an expert on herbal medicine and treatments.
https://www.nicoleapelian.com/

Alan Kay
While he may resemble an albino Sasquatch, Alan is the real deal when it comes to survival and preparedness teaching.
https://www.history.com/shows/alone/cast/alan-kay

Survival Dispatch
Whatever survival or preparedness topic you want covered, Survival Dispatch has it. The Insider membership is well worth it as well.
https://survivaldispatch.com/

Gardner Scott
If you want to get the most out of your garden, Scott can show you how.
https://gardenerscott.com/index.html

Articles on EMP Proof Vehicles
https://www.survivopedia.com/
best-emp-bug-out-vehicles/
https://www.shtfdad.com/how-to-emp-proof-your-car/

FIRST AID INFO, SUPPLIES, & TRAINING

https://www.doomandbloom.net/
http://www.skinnymedic.com/
https://www.redcross.org/
https://www.narescue.com/

AUTO REPAIR AND MAINTENANCE MANUALS

Haynes Manuals
https://haynes.com/en-us/

Chilton Manuals
https://www.chiltondiy.com/

AllData DIY
http://alldatadiy.com/index.html

AutoRepairManuals.com
https://www.auto-repair-manuals.com/

HIKING TRAILS / NATIONAL PARKS / MAPS

Getting out on our nation's trails and into our nation's forests and parks can be a great way to bond with your family, work on physical fitness, and practice all those survival and preparedness skills and plans you have been reading and gearing up for all these years. There's nothing like grabbing your bug-out bag and heading out into the woods for a dry run of how prepared you are (or think you are).

All Trails
One of the best websites for finding out all the trails near you and across the US. Great descriptions and reviews to help you plan your next outdoor adventure.
https://www.alltrails.com/

US Forest Service
A great place to find all the info you need to visit our nation's forests.
https://www.fs.usda.gov/

National Park Service
Find out about all the programs and benefits that the NPS has to offer.
https://www.nps.gov/index.htm

United States Geological Service
Land navigation is an essential skill that all preppers need to have. You'll find every kind of map you can imagine on this website.
https://www.usgs.gov/products/maps/overview

FEMA RESOURCES

They are the villain in a lot of stories, but they manage to do a few things right. Check out some of the resources available.

FEMA Storm Shelter Plans
https://www.fema.gov/emergency-managers/risk-management/safe-rooms

FEMA Grants

https://www.fema.gov/grants

FEMA Preparedness Courses
https://www.firstrespondertraining.gov/frts/npcc

C.E.R.T. INFO

If you haven't already done so, strongly consider joining your local CERT team. The connections and training available are well worth the time investment, as well as being able to help your community during times of disaster.

https://www.ready.gov/cert
https://community.fema.gov/Register/
Register_Search_Programs
https://training.fema.gov/nims/

NATIONAL PREPAREDNESS MONTH INFO

https://www.ready.gov/
september#:~:text=National%20Prepared-
ness%20Month%20(NPM)%20is,Make%20
Your%20Plan%20Today.%22

TAX FREE HOLIDAY INFO

Here is some info on the various tax free holidays. From preparedness to back to school products, these are the days to stock up.

https://blog.taxjar.com/2020-sales-tax-holidays/

HOTEL LOYALTY PROGRAMS

If you do a lot of traveling for business or other reasons, make sure to take advantage of all the benefits available.

https://thepointsguy.com/guide/
best-hotel-loyalty-programs/
https://thepointsguy.com/news/
how-to-decide-best-hotel-loyalty-program/
https://wallethub.com/edu/
best-hotel-rewards-program/25939/

HOME STORAGE TIPS FOR PREPPERS

You don't have to have a mansion to store all your prepper inventory. Here are some tips for maximizing the space you have.

https://survivalistprepper.net/
organization-storage-ideas-preppers/
https://www.goodhousekeeping.com/home/
organizing/g4226/bulk-shopper-organization-ideas/
https://theprovidentprepper.org/
ingenious-places-to-store-your-emergency-food-supply/
https://apartmentprepper.com/small-space-
prepping-25-ideas-for-stashing-your-stockpile/
https://momwithaprep.
com/50-organizing-tips-for-food-storage/

ANGERY AMERICAN INFO

This guide wouldn't be complete without some links to Chris Weatherman's books and products. Chris is legit and I'm honored to count him as a friend.

https://www.angeryamerican.tv/
https://www.patreon.com/user?u=28030776
https://www.facebook.com/AngeryAmerican/
https://survivaldispatch.com/author/chrisdispatch/

MONTHLY BUDGET TEMPLATE

Mortgage / Rent	$_____
Vehicle Payment	$_____
Auto Insurance	$_____
Medical Insurance	$_____
Groceries	$_____
Electric Bill	$_____
Gas Bill	$_____
Water Bill	$_____
Cell Phone Bill	$_____
Cable / Internet / Streaming Service Bill	$_____
Gasoline	$_____
Child Care / Tuition	$_____
Credit Card(s) Payment	$_____
Entertainment	$_____
Savings	$_____
_____ (Other)	$_____
_____ (Other)	$_____
_____ (Other)	$_____
Total	$_____
Balance	$_____

PREPAREDNESS GOALS

Check off each goal as it's completed.

Financial Preparedness	Complete
Balanced Monthly Budget	_____
$1000 Emergency Savings Account	_____
Savings to Cover One Month's Expenses	_____
Savings to Cover Six Month's Expenses	_____
Savings to Cover One Year's Expenses	_____
Vehicle(s) Paid Off	_____
Credit Card(s) Paid Off	_____
Mortgage Paid Off	_____
Food / Water Preparedness	**Complete**
Three Day Emergency Supply	_____
Two Week Emergency Supply	_____
One Month Emergency Supply	_____
Six Month Emergency Supply	_____
One Year Emergency Supply	_____

Emergency Evacuation Plans	Complete
Fire Escape Plan	_____
Inclement Weather Plan	_____
Emergency Meetup / Communication Plan	_____
Bug Out Plan	_____

HOME / VEHICLE SUPPLIES CHECKLIST

See Survival Dispatch for lists and articles / videos to help you obtain the gear and items necessary to complete your preps

Home Preps	Complete
3-Day Emergency Kit	_____
Bug Out Bag (1 for each family member)	_____
Comprehensive First Aid Kit	_____
90-Day Prescription Supply	_____
Emergency Cash (a few hundred dollars in small bills)	_____
Copies of Important Papers on Flash Drive	_____
Home Security Upgrades	_____

Self Defense Options (Firearms, Less Lethal, Etc.)	_____
Comprehensive Tool Kit	_____
Instructions for Home Shutdown (Power, Gas, Etc.)	_____
Source of Backup Power (Solar, Generator, Etc.)	_____
Vehicle Preps	**Complete**
Extra Fuel Supply	_____
Vehicle Tool Kit	_____
Proper Spare Tire(s)	_____
Get Home Bag (1 for each vehicle)	_____
Recovery Gear	_____
Extra Common Vehicle Parts (Filters, belts, hoses, etc.)	_____

VEHICLE MAINTENANCE LOG

Use this template to track your vehicle's maintenance intervals.

Service	Completion Date
Tire Rotation	_____
Tire Replacement	_____
Alignment	_____
Serpentine Belt	_____
Water Pump	_____
Spark Plugs / Wires	_____
Oil Change	_____
Transmission Flush / Filter Change	_____
Coolant Flush	_____
Air Conditioning Service	_____

ONE YEAR PREPAREDNESS INVENTORY LOG

Week #	Item(s) Purchased	Storage Location
1		
2		
3		
4		
5		
6		
7		
8		
9		
10		
11		
12		
13		
14		
15		

Week #	Item(s) Purchased	Storage Location
16		
17		
18		
19		
20		
21		
22		
23		
24		
25		
26		
27		
28		
29		
30		
31		

Week #	Item(s) Purchased	Storage Location
32		
33		
34		
35		
36		
37		
38		
39		
40		
41		
42		
43		
44		
45		
46		
47		

Week #	Item(s) Purchased	Storage Location
48		
49		
50		
51		
52		

NOTES

NOTES

NOTES

NOTES

NOTES